My Year of Seeking God

Name

Date

Given by

In the morning, Lord, you hear my voice;
in the morning I lay my requests before you
and wait expectantly.

Psalm 5:3

Olde Providence Press

All Scripture quotations, unless otherwise indicated, are taken from the Holy Bible, New International Version®, NIV®. Copyright ©1973, 1978, 1984, 2011 by Biblica, Inc.™ Used by permission of Zondervan. All rights reserved worldwide. www.zondervan.com The "NIV" and "New International Version" are trademarks registered in the United States Patent and Trademark Office by Biblica, Inc.™

Scripture quotations taken from the New American Standard Bible® (NASB),Copyright © 1960, 1962, 1963, 1968, 1971, 1972, 1973,1975, 1977, 1995 by The Lockman FoundationUsed by permission. www.Lockman.org"

"Northern Fields Collection" copyright Anastezia Luneva via Creative Market
"Eucalyptus & Lavender Frame Clip Art" copyright WonderWonder via Creative Market
"Silver South Font Duo" copyright Sam Parrett via Creative Market

Special thanks to Evan M., who sent so many Biblical promises. Evan, God is faithful to every one!

ISBN: 978-0-9854373-8-1

To the Father,
Who loved us while we were yet lost,
and to Jesus,
Who rescued us and brought us home.

*Call to me and I will answer you and tell you
great and unsearchable things you do not know.*
Jeremiah 33:3

How to Use This Journal

Scripture Promise

The Bible is filled with an inheritance of promises. As believers, we can be confident that God will honor every one. (See 2 Corinthians 1:20). Living a life based on the promises of God is a powerful way to live! Each week of this book starts with a new promise. Consider the unique and precious gift God is offering through the promise. Start your week remembering God's goodness and faithfulness.

Gratitude and Petitions

Philippians 4:6 teaches us to bring our concerns and petitions to the Lord *"in prayer and thanksgiving."* By taking time to consider ways that God has blessed you, you'll see that He is worthy of your trust. On this page, journal the ways that God has blessed you during the week. Then, prayerfully write anything that concerns you... anything at all! Nothing is too insignificant for God because He cares for you! There is also a space to write down the names of anyone you know needing prayer.

How to Use This Journal

Listening

When we pray, sometimes we forget to create a space for God to respond through the Holy Spirit. God speaks in many ways, but we are often too busy or distracted to hear His still small voice. In this space, journal as the Spirit leads you. In the box on the right, you'll see a Biblical list of the ways in which God communicates to us. Place a check mark next to the one that matches how God spoke to you during this time. The Scripture in the box on the right reminds us that still speaks today!

Whoever is united with the Lord is one with him in spirit.

1 Corinthians 6:17

Today God spoke to me through:

☐ Jesus
☐ Scripture
☐ Holy Spirit (Still Small Voice)
☐ Circumstances
☐ Creation
☐ Dreams & Visions
☐ Believers (People)
☐ Praise & Worship

Confirming through Scripture

List Bible verses that agree: Do any conflict? ☐ Yes ☐ No

My response:

Actions to take:

God's faithfulness ... Revealed!

Confirming through Scripture

The message you receive during your quiet time through the Holy Spirit will never contradict Scripture. In fact, Scripture is the *litmus test* for confirming that you have accurately heard God speak! It's imperative to take what you have journaled to Scripture and ask God to confirm it through His Word. Do any verses confirm the communication you received? Can you find any that contradict it? Seek the Bible and discover what it says. You'll find that the Holy Spirit, our Comforter and Advocate, will communicate with us in perfect agreement with His written Word.

How to Use This Journal

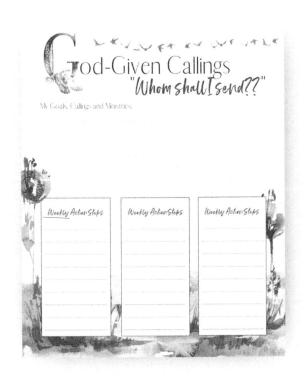

God-Given Callings

The Father wants to lead you every day. He has a plan and purpose for your life! When you seek Him, He will reveal the things He wants you to do. This can be a calling, a dream, a ministry, an act of kindness or forgiveness. In this space, record any steps that God, through the Holy Spirit, is calling you to do. Then prayerfully ask Him to lead you into His perfect will.

Weekly Planner

Living your best life is all about putting God first, and that means inviting Him into your schedule. As you draw near to God, you will have more peace in your life. He may ask you to remove activities from your schedule, or He may add something to it. Jesus says, "For my yoke is easy and my burden is light." (Matthew 11:30). Trust Him as you plan out your activities in the weekly planner pages.

God is Still Speaking

One of the most often-asked questions is, *"Does God still speak today?"*

My resounding answer is, "Yes, God still speaks to us!" The Father draws us into a relationship with Him through His Son, Jesus. In fact, God longs to communicate with His children: *"Call to me and I will answer you and tell you great and unsearchable things you do not know."* (Jeremiah 33:3).

If you doubt this truth still applies in today's world, consider the words of Jesus, "The Advocate, the Holy Spirit, whom the Father will send in my name, will teach you all things and will remind you of everything I have said to you." (John 14:26)

Jesus provides the answer to the question: *"I have much more to say to you, more than you can now bear. But when he, the Spirit of truth, comes, he will guide you into all the truth. He will not speak on his own; he will speak only what he hears, and he will tell you what is yet to come. He will glorify me because it is from me that he will receive what he will make known to you. All that belongs to the Father is mine. That is why I said the Spirit will receive from me what he will make known to you."* (John 16:12-15)

God, through Jesus, the Holy Spirit and Scripture, wants to lead us daily. He has promised never to leave us to fend for ourselves. He wants to be our guide. Jesus, His Son, wants to shepherd us to an abundant, full life. (John 10:10) This is His will for us… but are we listening to His direction or are we missing out?

Often the continual noise around us prevents us from hearing what He is saying. We are so slammed with busyness. Even if we hear His still, small voice, we rarely know what to do with the message. How do we sift the sweet words of the Spirit from the clammer and clatter around us? How do we know it's really God speaking?

This book will guide you through a process to help you. For 52 weeks, you'll learn to approach the throne boldly, allowing time to listen for God to speak to you. After a quiet period of journaling what you hear, you'll go to Scripture to confirm it. You will learn to recognize the voice of God and learn His ways. This book will change your life because it will be written in the time you spend alone with God. Ready to get started?

The Bible is the litmus test of anything you hear. Remember, God will never contradict His Word!

2020
AT-A-GLANCE

JANUARY

S	M	T	W	T	F	S
		01	02	03	04	
05	06	07	08	09	10	11
12	13	14	15	16	17	18
19	20	21	22	23	24	25
26	27	28	29	30	31	

_____
_____
_____
_____
_____

FEBRUARY

S	M	T	W	T	F	S
						01
02	03	04	05	06	07	08
09	10	11	12	13	14	15
16	17	18	19	20	21	22
23	24	25	26	27	28	29

_____
_____
_____
_____
_____

MARCH

S	M	T	W	T	F	S
01	02	03	04	05	06	07
08	09	10	11	12	13	14
15	16	17	18	19	20	21
22	23	24	25	26	27	28
29	30	31				

_____
_____
_____
_____
_____

APRIL

S	M	T	W	T	F	S
		01	02	03	04	
05	06	07	08	09	10	11
12	13	14	15	16	17	18
19	20	21	22	23	24	25
26	27	28	29	30		

_____
_____
_____
_____

MAY

S	M	T	W	T	F	S
					01	02
03	04	05	06	07	08	09
10	11	12	13	14	15	16
17	18	19	20	21	22	23
24	25	26	27	28	29	30
31						

_____
_____
_____
_____

JUNE

S	M	T	W	T	F	S
	01	02	03	04	05	06
07	08	09	10	11	12	13
14	15	16	17	18	19	20
21	22	23	24	25	26	27
28	29	30				

_____
_____
_____
_____

2020
AT-A-GLANCE

JULY

S	M	T	W	T	F	S
			01	02	03	04
05	06	07	08	09	10	11
12	13	14	15	16	17	18
19	20	21	22	23	24	25
26	27	28	29	30	31	

_____
_____
_____
_____
_____

AUGUST

S	M	T	W	T	F	S
						01
02	03	04	05	06	07	08
09	10	11	12	13	14	15
16	17	18	19	20	21	22
23	24	25	26	27	28	29
30	31					

_____
_____
_____
_____
_____

SEPTEMBER

S	M	T	W	T	F	S
		01	02	03	04	05
06	07	08	09	10	11	12
13	14	15	16	17	18	19
20	21	22	23	24	25	26
27	28	29	30			

_____
_____
_____
_____
_____

OCTOBER

S	M	T	W	T	F	S
				01	02	03
04	05	06	07	08	09	10
11	12	13	14	15	16	17
18	19	20	21	22	23	24
25	26	27	28	29	30	31

_____
_____
_____
_____
_____

NOVEMBER

S	M	T	W	T	F	S
01	02	03	04	05	06	07
08	09	10	11	12	13	14
15	16	17	18	19	20	21
22	23	24	25	26	27	28
29	30					

_____
_____
_____
_____
_____

DECEMBER

S	M	T	W	T	F	S
		01	02	03	04	05
06	07	08	09	10	11	12
13	14	15	16	17	18	19
20	21	22	23	24	25	26
27	28	29	30	31		

_____
_____
_____
_____
_____

Scripture Promise

You will seek me and find
me when you seek me with
all your heart.

Jeremiah 29:13

Week of:

I'm thankful for: My petitions & requests:

People on my mind:

Promise-Based Living:

For no matter how many promises God has made,
they are "Yes" in Christ. And so through him the
"Amen" is spoken by us to the glory of God.

2 Corinthians 1:20

Listening ...

My sheep listen to
my voice;
I know them, and they
follow me.

John 10:27

Today God spoke to me through:

☐ Jesus

☐ Scripture

☐ Holy Spirit (Still Small Voice)

☐ Circumstances

☐ Creation

☐ Dreams & Visions

☐ Believers (People)

☐ Praise & Worship

Confirming through Scripture

List Bible verses that agree: Do any conflict? ☐ Yes ☐ No

My response:

Actions to take:

God's faithfulness ... Revealed!

God-Given Callings
"Whom shall I send??"

My Goals, Callings and Ministries:

Weekly Action Steps	Weekly Action Steps	Weekly Action Steps

Weekly Planner

Week of: _____

SUNDAY

MONDAY

TUESDAY

WEDNESDAY

THURSDAY

FRIDAY

SATURDAY

to-do

notes

Scripture Promise

We know that in all things
God works for the good of
those who love him, who
have been called according
to his purpose.

Romans 8:28

Week of:

I'm thankful for:

My petitions & requests:

People on my mind:

Promise-Based Living:

Cast your cares on the Lord and he will sustain
you; he will never let the righteous be shaken.

Psalm 55:22

Listening ...

> For the Spirit God gave us does not make us timid, but gives us power, love and self-discipline.
>
> 2 Timothy 1:7

Today God spoke to me through:

- ☐ Jesus
- ☐ Scripture
- ☐ Holy Spirit (Still Small Voice)
- ☐ Circumstances
- ☐ Creation
- ☐ Dreams & Visions
- ☐ Believers (People)
- ☐ Praise & Worship

Confirming through Scripture

List Bible verses that agree: Do any conflict? ☐ Yes ☐ No

My response:

Actions to take:

God's faithfulness ... Revealed!

God-Given Callings
"Whom shall I send??"

My Goals, Callings and Ministries:

Weekly Action Steps	*Weekly Action Steps*	*Weekly Action Steps*
_____	_____	_____
_____	_____	_____
_____	_____	_____
_____	_____	_____
_____	_____	_____
_____	_____	_____
_____	_____	_____
_____	_____	_____

Weekly Planner

Week of: _____

SUNDAY

MONDAY

TUESDAY

WEDNESDAY

THURSDAY

FRIDAY

SATURDAY

to-do

notes

Scripture Promise

You, dear children, are from God and have overcome them, because the one who is in you is greater than the one who is in the world.

1 John 4:4

Week of:

I'm thankful for:

My petitions & requests:

People on my mind:

Promise-Based Living:

I sought the Lord, and he answered me; he delivered me from all my fears.

Psalm 34:4

Listening ...

> Rejoice always, pray continually, give thanks in all circumstances; for this is God's will for you in Christ Jesus.
>
> 1 Thessalonians 5:16-18

Today God spoke to me through:

- ☐ Jesus
- ☐ Scripture
- ☐ Holy Spirit (Still Small Voice)
- ☐ Circumstances
- ☐ Creation
- ☐ Dreams & Visions
- ☐ Believers (People)
- ☐ Praise & Worship

Confirming through Scripture

List Bible verses that agree: Do any conflict? ☐ Yes ☐ No

My response:

Actions to take:

God's faithfulness... Revealed!

God-Given Callings
"Whom shall I send??"

My Goals, Callings and Ministries:

Weekly Action Steps	Weekly Action Steps	Weekly Action Steps

Weekly Planner

Week of: _____

SUNDAY

MONDAY

TUESDAY

WEDNESDAY

THURSDAY

FRIDAY

SATURDAY

to-do

notes

 cripture Promise

Ah, Sovereign Lord, you have made the heavens and the earth by your great power and outstretched arm. Nothing is too hard for you.

Jeremiah 32:17

Week of:

I'm thankful for: My petitions & requests:

People on my mind:

Promise-Based Living:

If any of you lacks wisdom, you should ask God, who gives generously to all without finding fault, and it will be given to you.

James 1:5

Listening ...

Rejoice always, pray continually, give thanks in all circumstances; for this is God's will for you in Christ Jesus.

1 Thessalonians 5:16-18

Today God spoke to me through:

☐ Jesus
☐ Scripture
☐ Holy Spirit (Still Small Voice)
☐ Circumstances
☐ Creation
☐ Dreams & Visions
☐ Believers (People)
☐ Praise & Worship

Confirming *through Scripture*

List Bible verses that agree: Do any conflict? ☐ Yes ☐ No

My response:

Actions to take:

God's faithfulness ... Revealed!

God-Given Callings
"Whom shall I send??"

My Goals, Callings and Ministries:

Weekly Action Steps	Weekly Action Steps	Weekly Action Steps

Weekly Planner

Week of:

SUNDAY

MONDAY

TUESDAY

WEDNESDAY

THURSDAY

FRIDAY

SATURDAY

to-do

notes

Scripture Promise

He will call on me, and I will answer him; I will be with him in trouble, I will deliver him and honor him. With long life I will satisfy him and show him my salvation.

Psalm 91:15-16

Week of:

I'm thankful for:

My petitions & requests:

People on my mind:

Promise-Based Living:

I lift up my eyes to the mountains—where does my help come from? My help comes from the Lord, the Maker of heaven and earth.

Psalm 121:1-2

Listening ...

He will not let your foot slip—he who watches over you will not slumber;

Psalm 121:3

Today God spoke to me through:

- ☐ Jesus
- ☐ Scripture
- ☐ Holy Spirit (Still Small Voice)
- ☐ Circumstances
- ☐ Creation
- ☐ Dreams & Visions
- ☐ Believers (People)
- ☐ Praise & Worship

Confirming through Scripture

List Bible verses that agree: Do any conflict? ☐ Yes ☐ No

My response:

Actions to take:

God's faithfulness ... Revealed!

God-Given Callings
"Whom shall I send??"

My Goals, Callings and Ministries:

Weekly Action Steps	Weekly Action Steps	Weekly Action Steps
_____	_____	_____
_____	_____	_____
_____	_____	_____
_____	_____	_____
_____	_____	_____
_____	_____	_____
_____	_____	_____
_____	_____	_____

Weekly Planner

Week of: _____

SUNDAY

MONDAY

TUESDAY

WEDNESDAY

THURSDAY

FRIDAY

SATURDAY

to-do

notes

Scripture Promise

All have sinned and fall short of the glory of God, and all are justified freely by his grace through the redemption that came by Christ Jesus.

Romans 3:23-24

Week of:

I'm thankful for: My petitions & requests:

People on my mind:

Promise-Based Living:

God demonstrates His own love toward us,
in that while we were yet sinners,
Christ died for us.

Romans 5:8 (NASB)

Listening ...

Seek the Lord while he
may be found;
call on him while he
is near.

Isaiah 55:6

Today God spoke to me through:

☐ Jesus

☐ Scripture

☐ Holy Spirit (Still Small Voice)

☐ Circumstances

☐ Creation

☐ Dreams & Visions

☐ Believers (People)

☐ Praise & Worship

Confirming through Scripture

List Bible verses that agree: Do any conflict? ☐ Yes ☐ No

My response:

Actions to take:

God's faithfulness... Revealed!

God-Given Callings
"Whom shall I send??"

My Goals, Callings and Ministries:

Weekly Action Steps	Weekly Action Steps	Weekly Action Steps

Weekly Planner

Week of: _____

SUNDAY

MONDAY

TUESDAY

WEDNESDAY

THURSDAY

FRIDAY

SATURDAY

to-do

notes

Scripture Promise

As the heavens are higher than the earth, so are my ways higher than your ways and my thoughts than your thoughts.

Isaiah 55:9

Week of:

I'm thankful for:

My petitions & requests:

People on my mind:

Promise-Based Living:

Give ear and come to me; listen, that you may live.
I will make an everlasting covenant with you,
my faithful love promised to David.

Isaiah 55:3

Listening ...

> The eyes of
> the Lord are on the
> righteous,
> and his ears are
> attentive to their cry.
>
> Psalm 34:15

Today God spoke to me through:

- ☐ Jesus
- ☐ Scripture
- ☐ Holy Spirit (Still Small Voice)
- ☐ Circumstances
- ☐ Creation
- ☐ Dreams & Visions
- ☐ Believers (People)
- ☐ Praise & Worship

Confirming through Scripture

List Bible verses that agree: Do any conflict? ☐ Yes ☐ No

My response:

Actions to take:

God's faithfulness ... Revealed!

God-Given Callings
"Whom shall I send??"

My Goals, Callings and Ministries:

Weekly Action Steps	*Weekly Action Steps*	*Weekly Action Steps*
_____	_____	_____
_____	_____	_____
_____	_____	_____
_____	_____	_____
_____	_____	_____
_____	_____	_____
_____	_____	_____
_____	_____	_____
_____	_____	_____

Weekly Planner

Week of:

SUNDAY

MONDAY

TUESDAY

WEDNESDAY

THURSDAY

FRIDAY

SATURDAY

to-do

notes

Scripture Promise

Do you not know? Have you not heard? The Lord is the everlasting God, the Creator of the ends of the earth. He will not grow tired or weary, and his understanding no one can fathom.

Isaiah 40:28

Week of:

I'm thankful for:

My petitions & requests:

People on my mind:

Promise-Based Living:

Let us then approach God's throne of grace with confidence, so that we may receive mercy and find grace to help us in our time of need.

Hebrews 4:16

Listening ...

> Who, then, are those who fear the Lord? He will instruct them in the ways they should choose.
>
> Psalm 25:12

Today God spoke to me through:

☐ Jesus
☐ Scripture
☐ Holy Spirit (Still Small Voice)
☐ Circumstances
☐ Creation
☐ Dreams & Visions
☐ Believers (People)
☐ Praise & Worship

Confirming through Scripture

List Bible verses that agree: Do any conflict? ☐ Yes ☐ No

My response:

Actions to take:

God's faithfulness ... Revealed!

God-Given Callings
"Whom shall I send??"

My Goals, Callings and Ministries:

Weekly Action Steps	Weekly Action Steps	Weekly Action Steps

Weekly Planner

Week of: _____

SUNDAY

MONDAY

TUESDAY

WEDNESDAY

THURSDAY

FRIDAY

SATURDAY

to-do

notes

Scripture Promise

The Advocate, the Holy Spirit, whom the Father will send in my name, will teach you all things and will remind you of everything I have said to you.

John 14:26

Week of:

I'm thankful for:

My petitions & requests:

People on my mind:

Promise-Based Living:

Whether you turn to the right or to the left,
your ears will hear a voice behind you, saying,
"This is the way; walk in it."

Isaiah 30:21

Listening ...

Today, if you hear his voice, do not harden your hearts.

Hebrews 4:7

Today God spoke to me through:

- ☐ Jesus
- ☐ Scripture
- ☐ Holy Spirit (Still Small Voice)
- ☐ Circumstances
- ☐ Creation
- ☐ Dreams & Visions
- ☐ Believers (People)
- ☐ Praise & Worship

Confirming through Scripture

List Bible verses that agree: Do any conflict? ☐ Yes ☐ No

My response:

Actions to take:

God's faithfulness ... Revealed!

God-Given Callings
"Whom shall I send??"

My Goals, Callings and Ministries:

Weekly Action Steps	Weekly Action Steps	Weekly Action Steps

Weekly Planner

Week of: _____

SUNDAY

MONDAY

TUESDAY

WEDNESDAY

THURSDAY

FRIDAY

SATURDAY

to-do

notes

Scripture Promise

For the word of God is alive and active. Sharper than any double-edged sword, it penetrates even to dividing soul and spirit, joints and marrow; it judges the thoughts and attitudes of the heart.

Hebrews 4:12

Week of:

I'm thankful for:

My petitions & requests:

People on my mind:

Promise-Based Living:

Your word is a lamp for my feet,
a light on my path.

Psalm 119:105

Listening ...

You are my
hiding place and
my shield;
I wait for Your word.

Psalm 119:114

Today God spoke to me through:

- ☐ Jesus
- ☐ Scripture
- ☐ Holy Spirit (Still Small Voice)
- ☐ Circumstances
- ☐ Creation
- ☐ Dreams & Visions
- ☐ Believers (People)
- ☐ Praise & Worship

Confirming through Scripture

List Bible verses that agree: Do any conflict? ☐ Yes ☐ No

My response:

Actions to take:

God's faithfulness ... Revealed!

God-Given Callings

"Whom shall I send??"

My Goals, Callings and Ministries:

Weekly Action Steps	Weekly Action Steps	Weekly Action Steps

Weekly Planner

Week of: _____

SUNDAY

MONDAY

TUESDAY

WEDNESDAY

THURSDAY

FRIDAY

SATURDAY

to-do

notes

Scripture Promise

Behold, I am with you and will keep you wherever you go, and will bring you back to this land; for I will not leave you until I have done what I have promised you

Genesis 28:15 (NASB)

Week of:

I'm thankful for:

My petitions & requests:

People on my mind:

Promise-Based Living:

The Sovereign Lord has given me a well-instructed tongue, to know the word that sustains the weary. He wakens me morning by morning, wakens my ear to listen like one being instructed.

Isaiah 50:4

Listening ...

Then Jacob woke from his sleep and said, "Surely the LORD is in this place, and I did not know it."

Genesis 28:16 (NASB)

Today God spoke to me through:

- ☐ Jesus
- ☐ Scripture
- ☐ Holy Spirit (Still Small Voice)
- ☐ Circumstances
- ☐ Creation
- ☐ Dreams & Visions
- ☐ Believers (People)
- ☐ Praise & Worship

Confirming through Scripture

List Bible verses that agree: Do any conflict? ☐ Yes ☐ No

My response:

Actions to take:

God's faithfulness ... Revealed!

God-Given Callings
"Whom shall I send??"

My Goals, Callings and Ministries:

Weekly Action Steps	Weekly Action Steps	Weekly Action Steps

Weekly Planner

Week of: _____

SUNDAY

MONDAY

TUESDAY

WEDNESDAY

THURSDAY

FRIDAY

SATURDAY

to-do

notes

Scripture Promise

All Scripture is God-breathed and is useful for teaching, rebuking, correcting and training in righteousness, so that the servant of God may be thoroughly equipped for every good work.

2 Timothy 3:16-17

Week of:

I'm thankful for: My petitions & requests:

People on my mind:

 istening ...

For I am confident of this very thing, that He who began a good work in you will perfect it until the day of Christ Jesus.

Philippians 1:6 (NASB)

Today God spoke to me through:

☐ Jesus

☐ Scripture

☐ Holy Spirit (Still Small Voice)

☐ Circumstances

☐ Creation

☐ Dreams & Visions

☐ Believers (People)

☐ Praise & Worship

Confirming through Scripture

List Bible verses that agree: Do any conflict? ☐ Yes ☐ No

My response:

Actions to take:

God's faithfulness ... Revealed!

God-Given Callings

"Whom shall I send??"

My Goals, Callings and Ministries:

Weekly Action Steps	Weekly Action Steps	Weekly Action Steps

Weekly Planner

Week of: _____

SUNDAY

MONDAY

TUESDAY

WEDNESDAY

THURSDAY

FRIDAY

SATURDAY

to-do

notes

Scripture Promise

For whatever is hidden is meant to be disclosed, and whatever is concealed is meant to be brought out into the open. If anyone has ears to hear, let them hear.

Mark 4:22-23

Week of:

I'm thankful for: My petitions & requests:

People on my mind:

Promise-Based Living:

With many similar parables Jesus spoke the word to them, as much as they could understand.

Mark 4:33

Listening ...

It is the glory of God
to conceal a matter;
to search out a matter
is the glory of kings.

Proverbs 25:2

Today God spoke to me through:

☐ Jesus
☐ Scripture
☐ Holy Spirit (Still Small Voice)
☐ Circumstances
☐ Creation
☐ Dreams & Visions
☐ Believers (People)
☐ Praise & Worship

Confirming
through Scripture

List Bible verses that agree: Do any conflict? ☐ Yes ☐ No

My response:

Actions to take:

God's faithfulness ... Revealed!

God-Given Callings
"Whom shall I send??"

My Goals, Callings and Ministries:

Weekly Action Steps	Weekly Action Steps	Weekly Action Steps

Weekly Planner

Week of:

SUNDAY

MONDAY

TUESDAY

WEDNESDAY

THURSDAY

FRIDAY

SATURDAY

to-do

notes

Scripture Promise

Praise be to the God and Father of our Lord Jesus Christ, who has blessed us in the heavenly realms with every spiritual blessing in Christ.

Ephesians 1:3

Week of:

I'm thankful for:

My petitions & requests:

People on my mind:

Promise-Based Living:

You also were included in Christ when you heard the message of truth, the gospel of your salvation. When you believed, you were marked in him with a seal, the promised Holy Spirit

Ephesians 1:13

Listening ...

> Come, let us worship and bow down, Let us kneel before the LORD our Maker.
>
> Psalm 95:6

Today God spoke to me through:

- ☐ Jesus
- ☐ Scripture
- ☐ Holy Spirit (Still Small Voice)
- ☐ Circumstances
- ☐ Creation
- ☐ Dreams & Visions
- ☐ Believers (People)
- ☐ Praise & Worship

Confirming through Scripture

List Bible verses that agree: Do any conflict? ☐ Yes ☐ No

My response:

Actions to take:

God's faithfulness ... Revealed!

God-Given Callings
"Whom shall I send??"

My Goals, Callings and Ministries:

Weekly Action Steps	Weekly Action Steps	Weekly Action Steps

Weekly Planner

Week of: _____

SUNDAY

MONDAY

TUESDAY

WEDNESDAY

THURSDAY

FRIDAY

SATURDAY

to-do

notes

 # Scripture Promise

Who is the liar? It is whoever denies that Jesus is the Christ. Such a person is the antichrist—denying the Father and the Son.

1 John 2:22

Week of:

I'm thankful for: My petitions & requests:

People on my mind:

Promise-Based Living:

Put on the full armor of God, so that you can take
your stand against the devil's schemes.

Ephesians 6:11

Listening ...

Who is the liar? It is whoever denies that Jesus is the Christ. Such a person is the antichrist—denying the Father and the Son.

1 John 2:22

Today God spoke to me through:

☐ Jesus

☐ Scripture

☐ Holy Spirit (Still Small Voice)

☐ Circumstances

☐ Creation

☐ Dreams & Visions

☐ Believers (People)

☐ Praise & Worship

Confirming
through Scripture

List Bible verses that agree: Do any conflict? ☐ Yes ☐ No

My response:

Actions to take:

God's faithfulness ... Revealed!

God-Given Callings
"Whom shall I send??"

My Goals, Callings and Ministries:

Weekly Action Steps	Weekly Action Steps	Weekly Action Steps

Weekly Planner

Week of:

SUNDAY

MONDAY

TUESDAY

WEDNESDAY

THURSDAY

FRIDAY

SATURDAY

to-do

notes

 # Scripture Promise

But when he, the Spirit of truth, comes, he will guide you into all the truth. He will not speak on his own; he will speak only what he hears, and he will tell you what is yet to come.

John 16:13

Week of:

I'm thankful for:

My petitions & requests:

People on my mind:

Promise-Based Living:

All things that the Father has are Mine; therefore I said that He takes of Mine and will disclose it to you.

John 16:15 (NASB)

Listening ...

I have told you these things, so that in me you may have peace. In this world you will have trouble. But take heart! I have overcome the world.

John 16:33

Today God spoke to me through:

☐ Jesus
☐ Scripture
☐ Holy Spirit (Still Small Voice)
☐ Circumstances
☐ Creation
☐ Dreams & Visions
☐ Believers (People)
☐ Praise & Worship

Confirming throughScripture

List Bible verses that agree: Do any conflict? ☐ Yes ☐ No

My response:

Actions to take:

God's faithfulness ... Revealed!

God-Given Callings
"Whom shall I send??"

My Goals, Callings and Ministries:

Weekly Action Steps	Weekly Action Steps	Weekly Action Steps

Weekly Planner

Week of: _____

SUNDAY

MONDAY

TUESDAY

WEDNESDAY

THURSDAY

FRIDAY

SATURDAY

to-do

notes

 cripture Promise

What we have received is not the spirit of the world, but the Spirit who is from God, so that we may understand what God has freely given us.

1 Corinthians 2:12

Week of:

I'm thankful for: My petitions & requests:

People on my mind:

Promise-Based Living:

In the last days, God says, I will pour out my Spirit on all people. Your sons and daughters will prophesy, your young men will see visions, your old men will dream dreams.

Acts 2:17

Listening ...

Don't you know that you yourselves are God's temple and that God's Spirit dwells in your midst?

1 Corinthians 3:16

Today God spoke to me through:

☐ Jesus

☐ Scripture

☐ Holy Spirit (Still Small Voice)

☐ Circumstances

☐ Creation

☐ Dreams & Visions

☐ Believers (People)

☐ Praise & Worship

Confirming through Scripture

List Bible verses that agree: Do any conflict? ☐ Yes ☐ No

My response:

Actions to take:

God's faithfulness... Revealed!

God-Given Callings
"Whom shall I send??"

My Goals, Callings and Ministries:

Weekly Action Steps	Weekly Action Steps	Weekly Action Steps

Weekly Planner

Week of:

SUNDAY

MONDAY

TUESDAY

WEDNESDAY

THURSDAY

FRIDAY

SATURDAY

to-do

notes

cripture Promise

As his anointing teaches you about all things and as that anointing is real, not counterfeit—just as it has taught you, remain in him.

1 John 2:27

Week of:

I'm thankful for:

My petitions & requests:

People on my mind:

Promise-Based Living:

In him was life, and that life was the light of all mankind. The light shines in the darkness, and the darkness has not overcome! it.

John 1:4-5

Listening ...

In the beginning was the Word, and the Word was with God, and the Word was God.

John 1:1

Today God spoke to me through:

☐ Jesus
☐ Scripture
☐ Holy Spirit (Still Small Voice)
☐ Circumstances
☐ Creation
☐ Dreams & Visions
☐ Believers (People)
☐ Praise & Worship

Confirming through Scripture

List Bible verses that agree: Do any conflict? ☐ Yes ☐ No

My response:

Actions to take:

God's faithfulness ... Revealed!

God-Given Callings

"Whom shall I send??"

My Goals, Callings and Ministries:

Weekly Action Steps	Weekly Action Steps	Weekly Action Steps

Weekly Planner

Week of: _____

SUNDAY

MONDAY

TUESDAY

WEDNESDAY

THURSDAY

FRIDAY

SATURDAY

to-do

notes

Scripture Promise

You are all children of the light and children of the day. We do not belong to the night or to the darkness. So then, let us not be like others, who are asleep, but let us be awake and sober.

1 Thessalonians 5:5-6

Week of:

I'm thankful for: My petitions & requests:

People on my mind:

Promise-Based Living:

Rejoice always, pray continually, give thanks in all circumstances; for this is God's will for you in Christ Jesus.

1 Thessalonians 5:16-18

 Listening ...

> Do not quench the Spirit; Do not treat prophecies with contempt but test them all; hold on to what is good, reject every kind of evil.
>
> 1 Thessalonians 5:19-22

Today God spoke to me through:

- ☐ Jesus
- ☐ Scripture
- ☐ Holy Spirit (Still Small Voice)
- ☐ Circumstances
- ☐ Creation
- ☐ Dreams & Visions
- ☐ Believers (People)
- ☐ Praise & Worship

Confirming throughScripture

List Bible verses that agree: Do any conflict? ☐ Yes ☐ No

My response:

Actions to take:

God's faithfulness ... Revealed!

God-Given Callings
"Whom shall I send??"

My Goals, Callings and Ministries:

Weekly Action Steps	Weekly Action Steps	Weekly Action Steps

Weekly Planner

Week of: _____

SUNDAY

MONDAY

TUESDAY

WEDNESDAY

THURSDAY

FRIDAY

SATURDAY

to-do

notes

Scripture Promise

To all who did receive him, to those who believed in his name, he gave the right to become children of God — children born not of natural descent, nor of human decision or a husband's will, but born of God.

John 1:12-13

Week of: _____

I'm thankful for: My petitions & requests:

People on my mind:

Listening ...

For those who are led by the Spirit of God are the children of God.

Romans 8:14

Today God spoke to me through:

- ☐ Jesus
- ☐ Scripture
- ☐ Holy Spirit (Still Small Voice)
- ☐ Circumstances
- ☐ Creation
- ☐ Dreams & Visions
- ☐ Believers (People)
- ☐ Praise & Worship

Confirming
through Scripture

List Bible verses that agree: Do any conflict? ☐ Yes ☐ No

My response:

Actions to take:

God's faithfulness ... Revealed!

God-Given Callings

"Whom shall I send??"

My Goals, Callings and Ministries:

Weekly Action Steps	Weekly Action Steps	Weekly Action Steps
_____	_____	_____
_____	_____	_____
_____	_____	_____
_____	_____	_____
_____	_____	_____
_____	_____	_____
_____	_____	_____
_____	_____	_____

Weekly Planner

Week of: _____

SUNDAY

MONDAY

TUESDAY

WEDNESDAY

THURSDAY

FRIDAY

SATURDAY

to-do

notes

Scripture Promise

You made the heavens, even the highest heavens, and all their starry host, the earth and all that is on it, the seas and all that is in them. You give life to everything, and the multitudes of heaven worship you.

Nehemiah 9:6

Week of:

I'm thankful for:

My petitions & requests:

People on my mind:

Promise-Based Living:

For God does speak—now one way, now another—though no one perceives it. In a dream, in a vision of the night, when deep sleep falls on people as they slumber in their beds...

Job 33:14-15

Listening ...

> Before they call
> I will answer;
> while they are
> still speaking
> I will hear.
>
> Isaiah 65:24

Today God spoke to me through:

- ☐ Jesus
- ☐ Scripture
- ☐ Holy Spirit (Still Small Voice)
- ☐ Circumstances
- ☐ Creation
- ☐ Dreams & Visions
- ☐ Believers (People)
- ☐ Praise & Worship

Confirming through Scripture

List Bible verses that agree: Do any conflict? ☐ Yes ☐ No

My response:

Actions to take:

God's faithfulness ... Revealed!

God-Given Callings
"Whom shall I send??"

My Goals, Callings and Ministries:

Weekly Action Steps	*Weekly Action Steps*	*Weekly Action Steps*

Weekly Planner

Week of:

SUNDAY

MONDAY

TUESDAY

WEDNESDAY

THURSDAY

FRIDAY

SATURDAY

to-do

notes

 cripture Promise

So do not fear, for I am
with you; do not be dismayed,
for I am your God.
I will strengthen you and
help you; I will uphold you
with my righteous right hand.

Isaiah 41:10

Week of: _____

I'm thankful for:

My petitions & requests:

People on my mind:

Promise-Based Living:

I call upon the LORD, who is worthy to be praised,
And I am saved from my enemies.

Psalm 18:3 (NASB)

Listening ...

Cast all your anxiety on him because he cares for you.

1 Peter 5:7

Today God spoke to me through:

☐ Jesus

☐ Scripture

☐ Holy Spirit (Still Small Voice)

☐ Circumstances

☐ Creation

☐ Dreams & Visions

☐ Believers (People)

☐ Praise & Worship

Confirming through Scripture

List Bible verses that agree: Do any conflict? ☐ Yes ☐ No

My response:

Actions to take:

God's faithfulness ... Revealed!

God-Given Callings
"Whom shall I send??"

My Goals, Callings and Ministries:

Weekly Action Steps	Weekly Action Steps	Weekly Action Steps

Weekly Planner

Week of: _____

SUNDAY

MONDAY

TUESDAY

WEDNESDAY

THURSDAY

FRIDAY

SATURDAY

to-do

notes

Scripture Promise

But seek first his kingdom and his righteousness, and all these things will be given to you as well.

Matthew 6:33

Week of:

I'm thankful for:

My petitions & requests:

People on my mind:

Promise-Based Living:

The Lord looks down from heaven on all mankind to see if there are any who understand, any who seek God.

Psalm 14:2

Listening ...

The LORD is
good to those
who wait for Him,
To the person
who seeks Him.

Lamentations 3:25 (NASB)

Today God spoke to me through:

- ☐ Jesus
- ☐ Scripture
- ☐ Holy Spirit (Still Small Voice)
- ☐ Circumstances
- ☐ Creation
- ☐ Dreams & Visions
- ☐ Believers (People)
- ☐ Praise & Worship

Confirming through Scripture

List Bible verses that agree: Do any conflict?   ☐ Yes   ☐ No

My response:

Actions to take:

God's faithfulness ... Revealed!

God-Given Callings
"Whom shall I send??"

My Goals, Callings and Ministries:

Weekly Action Steps	Weekly Action Steps	Weekly Action Steps

Weekly Planner

Week of:

SUNDAY

MONDAY

TUESDAY

WEDNESDAY

THURSDAY

FRIDAY

SATURDAY

to-do

notes

Scripture Promise

Oh, the depth of the riches both of the wisdom and knowledge of God! How unsearchable are His judgments and unfathomable His ways!

Romans 11:33 (NASB)

Week of: _____

I'm thankful for: My petitions & requests:

People on my mind:

Promise-Based Living:

Let the wise listen and add to their learning, and let the discerning get guidance—for understanding proverbs and parables, the sayings and riddles of the wise.

Proverbs 1:5-6

Listening ...

Seek the LORD
and His strength;
Seek His face
continually.

1 Chronicles 16:11 (NASB)

Today God spoke to me through:

- ☐ Jesus
- ☐ Scripture
- ☐ Holy Spirit (Still Small Voice)
- ☐ Circumstances
- ☐ Creation
- ☐ Dreams & Visions
- ☐ Believers (People)
- ☐ Praise & Worship

Confirming through Scripture

List Bible verses that agree: Do any conflict? ☐ Yes ☐ No

My response:

Actions to take:

God's faithfulness ... Revealed!

God-Given Callings
"Whom shall I send??"

My Goals, Callings and Ministries:

Weekly Action Steps	Weekly Action Steps	Weekly Action Steps

Weekly Planner

Week of: _____

SUNDAY

MONDAY

TUESDAY

WEDNESDAY

THURSDAY

FRIDAY

SATURDAY

to-do

notes

Scripture Promise

I will ask the Father, and he will give you another advocate to help you and be with you forever— the Spirit of truth.

John 14:16-17

Week of: _____

I'm thankful for:

My petitions & requests:

People on my mind:

Promise-Based Living:

The world cannot accept him, because it neither sees him nor knows him. But you know him, for he lives with you and will be in you.

John 14:17

Listening ...

> Jesus answered, "I am the way and the truth and the life. No one comes to the Father except through me.
>
> John 14:6

Today God spoke to me through:

- ☐ Jesus
- ☐ Scripture
- ☐ Holy Spirit (Still Small Voice)
- ☐ Circumstances
- ☐ Creation
- ☐ Dreams & Visions
- ☐ Believers (People)
- ☐ Praise & Worship

Confirming
through Scripture

List Bible verses that agree: Do any conflict? ☐ Yes ☐ No

My response:

Actions to take:

God's faithfulness ... Revealed!

God-Given Callings
"Whom shall I send??"

My Goals, Callings and Ministries:

Weekly Action Steps	Weekly Action Steps	Weekly Action Steps

Weekly Planner

Week of:

SUNDAY

MONDAY

TUESDAY

WEDNESDAY

THURSDAY

FRIDAY

SATURDAY

to-do

notes

Scripture Promise

Therefore if anyone is in Christ, he is a new creature; the old things passed away; behold, new things have come.

2 Corinthians 5:17 (NASB)

Week of:

I'm thankful for:

My petitions & requests:

People on my mind:

Promise-Based Living:

For since the creation of the world God's invisible qualities—his eternal power and divine nature—have been clearly seen, being understood from what has been made, so that people are without excuse.

Romans 1:20

istening ...

> By the word of the Lord the heavens were made, their starry host by the breath of his mouth.
>
> Psalm 33:6

Today God spoke to me through:

- ☐ Jesus
- ☐ Scripture
- ☐ Holy Spirit (Still Small Voice)
- ☐ Circumstances
- ☐ Creation
- ☐ Dreams & Visions
- ☐ Believers (People)
- ☐ Praise & Worship

Confirming through Scripture

List Bible verses that agree: Do any conflict? ☐ Yes ☐ No

My response:

Actions to take:

God's faithfulness ... Revealed!

God-Given Callings
"Whom shall I send??"

My Goals, Callings and Ministries:

Weekly Action Steps
_____
_____
_____
_____
_____
_____
_____
_____
_____
_____

Weekly Action Steps
_____
_____
_____
_____
_____
_____
_____
_____
_____
_____

Weekly Action Steps
_____
_____
_____
_____
_____
_____
_____
_____
_____
_____

Weekly Planner

Week of: _____

SUNDAY

MONDAY

TUESDAY

WEDNESDAY

THURSDAY

FRIDAY

SATURDAY

to-do

notes

 cripture Promise

For everyone
who asks receives;
the one who seeks finds;
and to the one who knocks,
the door will be opened.

Matthew 7:8

Week of:

I'm thankful for: My petitions & requests:

People on my mind:

Promise-Based Living:
In the same way, the Spirit helps us in our
weakness. We do not know what we ought to pray for,
but the Spirit himself intercedes for us
through wordless groans.

Romans 8:26-27

Listening ...

> I waited patiently for the Lord; he turned to me and heard my cry.
>
> Psalm 40:1

Today God spoke to me through:

- ☐ Jesus
- ☐ Scripture
- ☐ Holy Spirit (Still Small Voice)
- ☐ Circumstances
- ☐ Creation
- ☐ Dreams & Visions
- ☐ Believers (People)
- ☐ Praise & Worship

Confirming through Scripture

List Bible verses that agree: Do any conflict? ☐ Yes ☐ No

My response:

Actions to take:

God's faithfulness ... Revealed!

God-Given Callings
"Whom shall I send??"

My Goals, Callings and Ministries:

Weekly Action Steps	Weekly Action Steps	Weekly Action Steps

Weekly Planner

Week of: _____

SUNDAY

MONDAY

TUESDAY

WEDNESDAY

THURSDAY

FRIDAY

SATURDAY

to-do

notes

Scripture Promise

Now the Lord is the Spirit,
and where
the Spirit of the Lord is,
there is freedom.

2 Corinthians 3:17

Week of:

I'm thankful for:

My petitions & requests:

People on my mind:

Promise-Based Living:

We all, who with unveiled faces contemplate the Lord's glory, are being transformed into his image with ever-increasing glory, which comes from the Lord, who is the Spirit.

2 Corinthians 3:18

Listening ...

Every good and perfect gift is from above, coming down from the Father of the heavenly lights, who does not change like shifting shadows.

James 1:17

Today God spoke to me through:

☐ Jesus
☐ Scripture
☐ Holy Spirit (Still Small Voice)
☐ Circumstances
☐ Creation
☐ Dreams & Visions
☐ Believers (People)
☐ Praise & Worship

Confirming through Scripture

List Bible verses that agree: Do any conflict? ☐ Yes ☐ No

My response:

Actions to take:

God's faithfulness ... Revealed!

God-Given Callings

"Whom shall I send??"

My Goals, Callings and Ministries:

Weekly Action Steps	Weekly Action Steps	Weekly Action Steps
_____	_____	_____
_____	_____	_____
_____	_____	_____
_____	_____	_____
_____	_____	_____
_____	_____	_____
_____	_____	_____
_____	_____	_____

Weekly Planner

Week of: _____

SUNDAY

MONDAY

TUESDAY

WEDNESDAY

THURSDAY

FRIDAY

SATURDAY

to-do

notes

Scripture Promise

Jesus came to them
and said, "All authority
in heaven and on earth
has been given to me..."

Matthew 28:18

Week of:

I'm thankful for: My petitions & requests:

People on my mind:

Promise-Based Living:
"Therefore go and make disciples of all nations,
baptizing them in the name of the Father and of the
Son and of the Holy Spirit and teaching them to obey
everything I have commanded you."
Matthew 28:19-20

Listening ...

> "Surely I am with you always, to the very end of the age."
>
> Matthew 28:20

Today God spoke to me through:

- ☐ Jesus
- ☐ Scripture
- ☐ Holy Spirit (Still Small Voice)
- ☐ Circumstances
- ☐ Creation
- ☐ Dreams & Visions
- ☐ Believers (People)
- ☐ Praise & Worship

Confirming *through Scripture*

List Bible verses that agree: Do any conflict? ☐ Yes ☐ No

My response:

Actions to take:

God's faithfulness ... Revealed!

God-Given Callings
"Whom shall I send??"

My Goals, Callings and Ministries:

Weekly Action Steps	Weekly Action Steps	Weekly Action Steps

Weekly Planner

Week of:

SUNDAY

MONDAY

TUESDAY

WEDNESDAY

THURSDAY

FRIDAY

SATURDAY

to-do

notes

Scripture Promise

For no matter how many promises God has made, they are "Yes" in Christ. And so through him the "Amen" is spoken by us to the glory of God.

2 Corinthians 1:20

Week of:

I'm thankful for: My petitions & requests:

People on my mind:

Promise-Based Living:

Now it is God who makes both us and you stand firm in Christ. He anointed us, set his seal of ownership on us, and put his Spirit in our hearts as a deposit, guaranteeing what is to come.

2 Corinthians 1:21-22

istening ...

> So we fix our eyes not on what is seen, but on what is unseen, since what is seen is temporary, but what is unseen is eternal.
>
> 2 Corinthians 4:18

Today God spoke to me through:

☐ Jesus

☐ Scripture

☐ Holy Spirit (Still Small Voice)

☐ Circumstances

☐ Creation

☐ Dreams & Visions

☐ Believers (People)

☐ Praise & Worship

Confirming through Scripture

List Bible verses that agree: Do any conflict? ☐ Yes ☐ No

My response:

Actions to take:

God's faithfulness ... Revealed!

God-Given Callings
"Whom shall I send??"

My Goals, Callings and Ministries:

Weekly Action Steps	Weekly Action Steps	Weekly Action Steps

Weekly Planner

Week of: _____

SUNDAY

MONDAY

TUESDAY

WEDNESDAY

THURSDAY

FRIDAY

SATURDAY

to-do

notes

Scripture Promise

If you belong to Christ, then you are Abraham's seed, and heirs according to the promise.

Galatians 3:29

Week of: _____

I'm thankful for: My petitions & requests:

People on my mind:

Promise-Based Living:

*I would have despaired unless I had believed
that I would see the goodness of the LORD
In the land of the living.*

Psalm 27:13-14 (NASB)

Listening ...

For we live by faith,
not by sight.

2 Corinthians 5:7

Today God spoke to me through:

☐ Jesus

☐ Scripture

☐ Holy Spirit (Still Small Voice)

☐ Circumstances

☐ Creation

☐ Dreams & Visions

☐ Believers (People)

☐ Praise & Worship

Confirming through Scripture

List Bible verses that agree: Do any conflict? ☐ Yes ☐ No

My response:

Actions to take:

God's faithfulness ... Revealed!

God-Given Callings
"Whom shall I send??"

My Goals, Callings and Ministries:

_____

Weekly Action Steps	Weekly Action Steps	Weekly Action Steps
_____	_____	_____
_____	_____	_____
_____	_____	_____
_____	_____	_____
_____	_____	_____
_____	_____	_____
_____	_____	_____
_____	_____	_____

Weekly Planner

Week of: _____

SUNDAY

MONDAY

TUESDAY

WEDNESDAY

THURSDAY

FRIDAY

SATURDAY

to-do

notes

Scripture Promise

Yet to all who did receive him, to those who believed in his name, he gave the right to become children of God

John 1:12

Week of:

I'm thankful for:

My petitions & requests:

People on my mind:

Listening ...

I press on toward the goal for the prize of the upward call of God in Christ Jesus.

Philippians 3:14 (NASB)

Today God spoke to me through:

☐ Jesus
☐ Scripture
☐ Holy Spirit (Still Small Voice)
☐ Circumstances
☐ Creation
☐ Dreams & Visions
☐ Believers (People)
☐ Praise & Worship

Confirming through Scripture

List Bible verses that agree: Do any conflict? ☐ Yes ☐ No

My response:

Actions to take:

God's faithfulness ... Revealed!

God-Given Callings
"Whom shall I send??"

My Goals, Callings and Ministries:

Weekly Action Steps	Weekly Action Steps	Weekly Action Steps

Weekly Planner

Week of: _____

SUNDAY

MONDAY

TUESDAY

WEDNESDAY

THURSDAY

FRIDAY

SATURDAY

to-do

notes

Scripture Promise

And now these
three remain:
faith, hope and love.
But the greatest of these
is love.

1 Corinthians 13:13

Week of:

I'm thankful for:

My petitions & requests:

People on my mind:

Promise-Based Living:

Do you not know that your bodies are temples
of the Holy Spirit, who is in you,
whom you have received from God?

1 Corinthians 6:19

Listening ...

Whoever is united with the Lord is one with him in spirit.

1 Corinthians 6:17

Today God spoke to me through:

- ☐ Jesus
- ☐ Scripture
- ☐ Holy Spirit (Still Small Voice)
- ☐ Circumstances
- ☐ Creation
- ☐ Dreams & Visions
- ☐ Believers (People)
- ☐ Praise & Worship

Confirming through Scripture

List Bible verses that agree: Do any conflict? ☐ Yes ☐ No

My response:

Actions to take:

God's faithfulness ... Revealed!

God-Given Callings
"Whom shall I send??"

My Goals, Callings and Ministries:

Weekly Action Steps	Weekly Action Steps	Weekly Action Steps

Weekly Planner

Week of:

SUNDAY

MONDAY

TUESDAY

WEDNESDAY

THURSDAY

FRIDAY

SATURDAY

to-do

notes

Scripture Promise

I keep asking that
the God of our Lord Jesus
Christ, the glorious Father,
may give you the Spirit of
wisdom and revelation, so that
you may know him better.

Ephesians 1:17

Week of:

I'm thankful for:

My petitions & requests:

People on my mind:

Promise-Based Living:

I pray that the eyes of your heart may be
enlightened in order that you may know the hope to
which he has called you, the riches of his glorious
inheritance in his holy people,

Ephesians 1:18

istening ...

> For you were once darkness, but now you are light in the Lord. Live as children of light
>
> Ephesians 5:8

Today God spoke to me through:

- ☐ Jesus
- ☐ Scripture
- ☐ Holy Spirit (Still Small Voice)
- ☐ Circumstances
- ☐ Creation
- ☐ Dreams & Visions
- ☐ Believers (People)
- ☐ Praise & Worship

Confirming
through Scripture

List Bible verses that agree: Do any conflict? ☐ Yes ☐ No

My response:

Actions to take:

God's faithfulness ... Revealed!

God-Given Callings
"Whom shall I send??"

My Goals, Callings and Ministries:

Weekly Action Steps	Weekly Action Steps	Weekly Action Steps

Weekly Planner

Week of: _____

SUNDAY

MONDAY

TUESDAY

WEDNESDAY

THURSDAY

FRIDAY

SATURDAY

to-do

notes

Scripture Promise

For I am confident
of this very thing,
that He who began
a good work in you
will perfect it until
the day of Christ Jesus.

Philippians 1:6 (NASB)

Week of:

I'm thankful for:

My petitions & requests:

People on my mind:

 Listening ...

> Guard, through the Holy Spirit who dwells in us, the treasure which has been entrusted to you.
>
> 2 Timothy 1:14 (NASB)

Today God spoke to me through:

- ☐ Jesus
- ☐ Scripture
- ☐ Holy Spirit (Still Small Voice)
- ☐ Circumstances
- ☐ Creation
- ☐ Dreams & Visions
- ☐ Believers (People)
- ☐ Praise & Worship

Confirming *through Scripture*

List Bible verses that agree: Do any conflict? ☐ Yes ☐ No

My response:

Actions to take:

God's faithfulness ... Revealed!

God-Given Callings
"Whom shall I send??"

My Goals, Callings and Ministries:

Weekly Action Steps	Weekly Action Steps	Weekly Action Steps

Weekly Planner

Week of: _____

SUNDAY

MONDAY

TUESDAY

WEDNESDAY

THURSDAY

FRIDAY

SATURDAY

to-do

notes

Scripture Promise

I will pray with my spirit, but I will also pray with my understanding; I will sing with my spirit, but I will also sing with my understanding.

1 Corinthians 14:15

Week of:

I'm thankful for: My petitions & requests:

People on my mind:

Promise-Based Living:

Pray in the Spirit on all occasions with all kinds of prayers and requests. With this in mind, be alert and always keep on praying for all the Lord's people.

Ephesians 6:18

Listening ...

> Therefore do not be foolish, but understand what the Lord's will is.
>
> Ephesians 5:17

Today God spoke to me through:

- ☐ Jesus
- ☐ Scripture
- ☐ Holy Spirit (Still Small Voice)
- ☐ Circumstances
- ☐ Creation
- ☐ Dreams & Visions
- ☐ Believers (People)
- ☐ Praise & Worship

Confirming through Scripture

List Bible verses that agree: Do any conflict? ☐ Yes ☐ No

My response:

Actions to take:

God's faithfulness ... Revealed!

God-Given Callings

"Whom shall I send??"

My Goals, Callings and Ministries:

Weekly Action Steps	Weekly Action Steps	Weekly Action Steps

Weekly Planner

Week of: _____

SUNDAY

MONDAY

TUESDAY

WEDNESDAY

THURSDAY

FRIDAY

SATURDAY

to-do

notes

Scripture Promise

As the heavens are
higher than the earth,
so are my ways higher than
your ways and my thoughts
than your thoughts.

Isaiah 55:9

Week of:

I'm thankful for:

My petitions & requests:

People on my mind:

Promise-Based Living:

For I know the plans I have for you," declares the Lord," plans to prosper you and not to harm you, plans to give you hope and a future.

Jeremiah 29:11

Listening ...

The tongue has the power of life and death, and those who love it will eat its fruit.

Proverbs 18:21

Today God spoke to me through:

☐ Jesus
☐ Scripture
☐ Holy Spirit (Still Small Voice)
☐ Circumstances
☐ Creation
☐ Dreams & Visions
☐ Believers (People)
☐ Praise & Worship

Confirming through Scripture

List Bible verses that agree: Do any conflict? ☐ Yes ☐ No

My response:

Actions to take:

God's faithfulness ... Revealed!

God-Given Callings
"Whom shall I send??"

My Goals, Callings and Ministries:

Weekly Action Steps	Weekly Action Steps	Weekly Action Steps
_____	_____	_____
_____	_____	_____
_____	_____	_____
_____	_____	_____
_____	_____	_____
_____	_____	_____
_____	_____	_____
_____	_____	_____

Weekly Planner

Week of: _____

SUNDAY

MONDAY

TUESDAY

WEDNESDAY

THURSDAY

FRIDAY

SATURDAY

to-do

notes

Scripture Promise

"Truly I tell you, if anyone says to this mountain, 'Go, throw yourself into the sea,' and does not doubt in their heart but believes that what they say will happen, it will be done for them."

Mark 11:23

Week of:

I'm thankful for:

My petitions & requests:

People on my mind:

Promise-Based Living:

"Whenever you stand praying, forgive, if you have anything against anyone, so that your Father who is in heaven will also forgive you your transgressions."

Mark 11:25 (NASB)

Listening ...

Trust in the Lord with all your heart and lean not on your own understanding; in all your ways submit to him, and he will make your paths straight.

Proverbs 3:5-6

Today God spoke to me through:

☐ Jesus

☐ Scripture

☐ Holy Spirit (Still Small Voice)

☐ Circumstances

☐ Creation

☐ Dreams & Visions

☐ Believers (People)

☐ Praise & Worship

Confirming through Scripture

List Bible verses that agree: Do any conflict? ☐ Yes ☐ No

My response:

Actions to take:

God's faithfulness ... Revealed!

God-Given Callings

"Whom shall I send??"

My Goals, Callings and Ministries:

Weekly Action Steps	Weekly Action Steps	Weekly Action Steps

Weekly Planner

Week of:

SUNDAY

MONDAY

TUESDAY

WEDNESDAY

THURSDAY

FRIDAY

SATURDAY

to-do

notes

 cripture Promise

The LORD will protect you from all evil; He will keep your soul. The LORD will guard your going out and your coming in from this time forth and forever.

Psalm 121:7-8 (NASB)

Week of:

I'm thankful for:

My petitions & requests:

People on my mind:

Promise-Based Living:

In my distress I called to the Lord; I cried to my God for help. From his temple he heard my voice; my cry came before him, into his ears.

Psalm 18:6

Listening ...

He brought me out into a spacious place; he rescued me because he delighted in me.

Psalm 18:19

Today God spoke to me through:

☐ Jesus

☐ Scripture

☐ Holy Spirit (Still Small Voice)

☐ Circumstances

☐ Creation

☐ Dreams & Visions

☐ Believers (People)

☐ Praise & Worship

Confirming
through Scripture

List Bible verses that agree: Do any conflict? ☐ Yes ☐ No

My response:

Actions to take:

God's faithfulness ... Revealed!

God-Given Callings
"Whom shall I send??"

My Goals, Callings and Ministries:

Weekly Action Steps	*Weekly Action Steps*	*Weekly Action Steps*
_____	_____	_____
_____	_____	_____
_____	_____	_____
_____	_____	_____
_____	_____	_____
_____	_____	_____
_____	_____	_____
_____	_____	_____

Weekly Planner

Week of: _____

SUNDAY

MONDAY

TUESDAY

WEDNESDAY

THURSDAY

FRIDAY

SATURDAY

to-do

notes

Scripture Promise

"I will give you the keys of the kingdom of heaven; and whatever you bind on earth shall have been bound in heaven, and whatever you loose on earth shall have been loosed in heaven."

Matthew 16:19 (NASB)

Week of: _____

I'm thankful for: My petitions & requests:

People on my mind:

Promise-Based Living:

Confess your sins to each other and pray for each other so that you may be healed. The prayer of a righteous person is powerful and effective.

James 5:16

Listening ...

Praise be to God,
who has not rejected
my prayer or
withheld his love
from me!

Psalm 66:20

Today God spoke to me through:

☐ Jesus
☐ Scripture
☐ Holy Spirit (Still Small Voice)
☐ Circumstances
☐ Creation
☐ Dreams & Visions
☐ Believers (People)
☐ Praise & Worship

Confirming through Scripture

List Bible verses that agree: Do any conflict? ☐ Yes ☐ No

My response:

Actions to take:

God's faithfulness ... Revealed!

God-Given Callings
"Whom shall I send??"

My Goals, Callings and Ministries:

Weekly Action Steps	Weekly Action Steps	Weekly Action Steps

Weekly Planner

Week of:

SUNDAY

MONDAY

TUESDAY

WEDNESDAY

THURSDAY

FRIDAY

SATURDAY

to-do

notes

Scripture Promise

You are a chosen people, a royal priesthood, a holy nation, God's special possession, that you may declare the praises of him who called you out of darkness into his wonderful light.

1 Peter 2:9

Week of:

I'm thankful for: My petitions & requests:

People on my mind:

Promise-Based Living:
Without faith it is impossible to please God,
because anyone who comes to him must believe
that he exists and that he rewards those who
earnestly seek him.
Hebrews 11:6

Listening ...

When you ask, you must believe and not doubt, because the one who doubts is like a wave of the sea, blown and tossed by the wind.

James 1:6

Today God spoke to me through:

☐ Jesus

☐ Scripture

☐ Holy Spirit (Still Small Voice)

☐ Circumstances

☐ Creation

☐ Dreams & Visions

☐ Believers (People)

☐ Praise & Worship

Confirming through Scripture

List Bible verses that agree: Do any conflict? ☐ Yes ☐ No

My response:

Actions to take:

God's faithfulness ... Revealed!

God-Given Callings

"Whom shall I send??"

My Goals, Callings and Ministries:

Weekly Action Steps	Weekly Action Steps	Weekly Action Steps

Weekly Planner

Week of:

SUNDAY

MONDAY

TUESDAY

WEDNESDAY

THURSDAY

FRIDAY

SATURDAY

to-do

notes

# Scripture Promise

Peace I leave with you; my peace I give you. I do not give to you as the world gives. Do not let your hearts be troubled and do not be afraid.

John 14:27

Week of:

I'm thankful for:

My petitions & requests:

People on my mind:

Promise-Based Living:

Jesus replied, "Anyone who loves me will obey my teaching. My Father will love them, and we will come to them and make our home with them."

John 14:23

Listening ...

"I am the vine; you are the branches. If you remain in me and I in you, you will bear much fruit; apart from me you can do nothing."

John 15:5

Today God spoke to me through:

☐ Jesus

☐ Scripture

☐ Holy Spirit (Still Small Voice)

☐ Circumstances

☐ Creation

☐ Dreams & Visions

☐ Believers (People)

☐ Praise & Worship

Confirming through Scripture

List Bible verses that agree: Do any conflict?   ☐ Yes   ☐ No

My response:

Actions to take:

God's faithfulness ... Revealed!

God-Given Callings
"Whom shall I send??"

My Goals, Callings and Ministries:

Weekly Action Steps	Weekly Action Steps	Weekly Action Steps

Weekly Planner

Week of:

SUNDAY

MONDAY

TUESDAY

WEDNESDAY

THURSDAY

FRIDAY

SATURDAY

to-do

notes

 # Scripture Promise

Since you are precious and honored in my sight, and because I love you, I will give people in exchange for you, nations in exchange for your life.

Isaiah 43:4

Week of:

I'm thankful for:

My petitions & requests:

People on my mind:

Promise-Based Living:

I no longer call you servants, because a servant does not know his master's business. Instead, I have called you friends, for everything that I learned from my Father I have made known to you.

John 15:15

Listening ...

> You have searched me, Lord, and you know me. You know when I sit and when I rise; you perceive my thoughts from afar.
>
> Psalm 139:1-2

Today God spoke to me through:

- ☐ Jesus
- ☐ Scripture
- ☐ Holy Spirit (Still Small Voice)
- ☐ Circumstances
- ☐ Creation
- ☐ Dreams & Visions
- ☐ Believers (People)
- ☐ Praise & Worship

Confirming through Scripture

List Bible verses that agree: Do any conflict? ☐ Yes ☐ No

My response:

Actions to take:

God's faithfulness ... Revealed!

God-Given Callings
"Whom shall I send??"

My Goals, Callings and Ministries:

Weekly Action Steps	Weekly Action Steps	Weekly Action Steps

Weekly Planner

Week of:

SUNDAY

MONDAY

TUESDAY

WEDNESDAY

THURSDAY

FRIDAY

SATURDAY

to-do

notes

Scripture Promise

You are altogether beautiful, my darling; there is no flaw in you.

Song of Solomon 4:7

Week of:

I'm thankful for:

My petitions & requests:

People on my mind:

Listening ...

In all these things we are more than conquerors through him who loved us.

Romans 8:37

Today God spoke to me through:

- ☐ Jesus
- ☐ Scripture
- ☐ Holy Spirit (Still Small Voice)
- ☐ Circumstances
- ☐ Creation
- ☐ Dreams & Visions
- ☐ Believers (People)
- ☐ Praise & Worship

Confirming through Scripture

List Bible verses that agree: Do any conflict? ☐ Yes ☐ No

My response:

Actions to take:

God's faithfulness ... Revealed!

God-Given Callings
"Whom shall I send??"

My Goals, Callings and Ministries:

Weekly Action Steps	Weekly Action Steps	Weekly Action Steps

Weekly Planner

Week of: _____

SUNDAY

MONDAY

TUESDAY

WEDNESDAY

THURSDAY

FRIDAY

SATURDAY

to-do

notes

 cripture Promise

Have I not commanded you?
Be strong and courageous.
Do not be afraid; do not be
discouraged, for the Lord your
God will be with you
wherever you go.

Joshua 1:9

Week of:

I'm thankful for: My petitions & requests:

People on my mind:

Promise-Based Living:

You know with all your heart and soul that not one of all the good promises the Lord your God gave you has failed. Every promise has been fulfilled; not one has failed.

Joshua 23:14

Listening ...

Come to me, all you who are weary and burdened, and I will give you rest.

Matthew 11:28

Today God spoke to me through:

☐ Jesus

☐ Scripture

☐ Holy Spirit (Still Small Voice)

☐ Circumstances

☐ Creation

☐ Dreams & Visions

☐ Believers (People)

☐ Praise & Worship

Confirming through Scripture

List Bible verses that agree: Do any conflict? ☐ Yes ☐ No

My response:

Actions to take:

God's faithfulness ... Revealed!

God-Given Callings
"Whom shall I send??"

My Goals, Callings and Ministries:

Weekly Action Steps	Weekly Action Steps	Weekly Action Steps

Weekly Planner

Week of: _____

SUNDAY

MONDAY

TUESDAY

WEDNESDAY

THURSDAY

FRIDAY

SATURDAY

to-do

notes

Scripture Promise

Let us be sober, putting on faith and love as a breastplate, and the hope of salvation as a helmet. For God did not appoint us to suffer wrath but to receive salvation through our Lord Jesus Christ.

1 Thessalonians 5:8-9

Week of:

I'm thankful for:

My petitions & requests:

People on my mind:

Promise-Based Living:

When you pray, go into your room, close the door
and pray to your Father, who is unseen.
Then your Father, who sees what is done in secret,
will reward you.

Matthew 6:6

Listening ...

The gatekeeper opens the gate for him, and the sheep listen to his voice. He calls his own sheep by name and leads them out.

John 10:3

Today God spoke to me through:

- ☐ Jesus
- ☐ Scripture
- ☐ Holy Spirit (Still Small Voice)
- ☐ Circumstances
- ☐ Creation
- ☐ Dreams & Visions
- ☐ Believers (People)
- ☐ Praise & Worship

Confirming through Scripture

List Bible verses that agree: Do any conflict? ☐ Yes ☐ No

My response:

Actions to take:

God's faithfulness ... Revealed!

God-Given Callings

"Whom shall I send??"

My Goals, Callings and Ministries:

Weekly Action Steps	Weekly Action Steps	Weekly Action Steps

Weekly Planner

Week of: _____

SUNDAY

MONDAY

TUESDAY

WEDNESDAY

THURSDAY

FRIDAY

SATURDAY

to-do

notes

# Scripture Promise

The Lord is my
light and my salvation—
whom shall I fear?
The Lord is the stronghold
of my life—of whom
shall I be afraid?

Psalm 27:1

Week of:

I'm thankful for:

My petitions & requests:

People on my mind:

Promise-Based Living:

One thing I ask from the Lord, this only do I seek: that I may dwell in the house of the Lord all the days of my life, to gaze on the beauty of the Lord and to seek him in his temple.

Psalm 27:4

Listening ...

Hear my voice
when I call, Lord;
be merciful to me
and answer me.

Psalm 27:7

Today God spoke to me through:

☐ Jesus
☐ Scripture
☐ Holy Spirit (Still Small Voice)
☐ Circumstances
☐ Creation
☐ Dreams & Visions
☐ Believers (People)
☐ Praise & Worship

Confirming *through Scripture*

List Bible verses that agree: Do any conflict? ☐ Yes ☐ No

My response:

Actions to take:

God's faithfulness ... Revealed!

God-Given Callings
"Whom shall I send??"

My Goals, Callings and Ministries:

Weekly Action Steps	Weekly Action Steps	Weekly Action Steps

Weekly Planner

Week of: _____

SUNDAY

MONDAY

TUESDAY

WEDNESDAY

THURSDAY

FRIDAY

SATURDAY

to-do

notes

God-Given Callings
"Whom shall I send??"

My Goals, Callings and Ministries:

Weekly Action Steps	Weekly Action Steps	Weekly Action Steps

Weekly Planner

Week of: _____

SUNDAY

MONDAY

TUESDAY

WEDNESDAY

THURSDAY

FRIDAY

SATURDAY

to-do

notes

Scripture Promise

In peace I will lie down
and sleep,
for you alone, Lord,
make me dwell in safety.

Psalm 4:3

Week of:

I'm thankful for: My petitions & requests:

People on my mind:

Promise-Based Living:

"I am the Lord your God, who brought you out of
Egypt, out of the land of slavery. You shall have
no other gods before me."

Exodus 20:1-3

Listening ...

Know that the Lord has set apart his faithful servant for himself; the Lord hears when I call to him.

Psalm 4:3

Today God spoke to me through:

- ☐ Jesus
- ☐ Scripture
- ☐ Holy Spirit (Still Small Voice)
- ☐ Circumstances
- ☐ Creation
- ☐ Dreams & Visions
- ☐ Believers (People)
- ☐ Praise & Worship

Confirming through Scripture

List Bible verses that agree: Do any conflict? ☐ Yes ☐ No

My response:

Actions to take:

God's faithfulness ... Revealed!

God-Given Callings
"Whom shall I send??"

My Goals, Callings and Ministries:

Weekly Action Steps

_____
_____
_____
_____
_____
_____
_____
_____

Weekly Action Steps

_____
_____
_____
_____
_____
_____
_____
_____

Weekly Action Steps

_____
_____
_____
_____
_____
_____
_____
_____

Weekly Planner

Week of:

SUNDAY

MONDAY

TUESDAY

WEDNESDAY

THURSDAY

FRIDAY

SATURDAY

to-do

notes

 cripture Promise

He will yet fill your mouth with laughter and your lips with shouts of joy. Your enemies will be clothed in shame, and the tents of the wicked will be no more.

Job 8:21-22

Week of:

I'm thankful for:

My petitions & requests:

People on my mind:

Promise-Based Living:

The thief comes only to steal and kill and destroy; I have come that they may have life, and have it to the full.

John 10:10

Listening ...

Blessed are you who hunger now, for you will be satisfied. Blessed are you who weep now, for you will laugh.

Luke 6:21

Today God spoke to me through:

☐ Jesus

☐ Scripture

☐ Holy Spirit (Still Small Voice)

☐ Circumstances

☐ Creation

☐ Dreams & Visions

☐ Believers (People)

☐ Praise & Worship

Confirming through Scripture

List Bible verses that agree: Do any conflict?   ☐ Yes ☐ No

My response:

Actions to take:

God's faithfulness ... Revealed!

God-Given Callings
"Whom shall I send??"

My Goals, Callings and Ministries:

Weekly Action Steps	Weekly Action Steps	Weekly Action Steps

Weekly Planner

Week of:

SUNDAY

MONDAY

TUESDAY

WEDNESDAY

THURSDAY

FRIDAY

SATURDAY

to-do

notes

Scripture Promise

For the Lord is good and his love endures forever; his faithfulness continues through all generations.

Psalm 100:5

Week of:

I'm thankful for:

My petitions & requests:

People on my mind:

Promise-Based Living:

Many false prophets will appear and deceive many people. Because of the increase of wickedness, the love of most will grow cold, but the one who stands firm to the end will be saved.

Matthew 24:11-13

 Listening ...

> Simon Peter answered him, "Lord, to whom shall we go? You have the words of eternal life."
>
> John 6:68

Today God spoke to me through:

- ☐ Jesus
- ☐ Scripture
- ☐ Holy Spirit (Still Small Voice)
- ☐ Circumstances
- ☐ Creation
- ☐ Dreams & Visions
- ☐ Believers (People)
- ☐ Praise & Worship

Confirming through Scripture

List Bible verses that agree: Do any conflict? ☐ Yes ☐ No

My response:

Actions to take:

God's faithfulness ... Revealed!

God-Given Callings
"Whom shall I send??"

My Goals, Callings and Ministries:

Weekly Action Steps	Weekly Action Steps	Weekly Action Steps

Weekly Planner

Week of:

SUNDAY

MONDAY

TUESDAY

WEDNESDAY

THURSDAY

FRIDAY

SATURDAY

to-do

notes

Scripture Promise

See, I have engraved you on the palms of my hands; your walls are ever before me.

Isaiah 49:16

Week of:

I'm thankful for:

My petitions & requests:

People on my mind:

Promise-Based Living:

The Lord your God is with you, the Mighty Warrior who saves. He will take great delight in you; in his love he will no longer rebuke you, but will rejoice over you with singing.

Zephaniah 3:17

istening ...

I have made Your name known to them, and will make it known, so that the love with which You loved Me may be in them, and I in them.

John 17:26 (NASB)

Today God spoke to me through:

☐ Jesus

☐ Scripture

☐ Holy Spirit (Still Small Voice)

☐ Circumstances

☐ Creation

☐ Dreams & Visions

☐ Believers (People)

☐ Praise & Worship

Confirming through Scripture

List Bible verses that agree: Do any conflict? ☐ Yes ☐ No

My response:

Actions to take:

God's faithfulness ... Revealed!

God-Given Callings
"Whom shall I send??"

My Goals, Callings and Ministries:

Weekly Action Steps	Weekly Action Steps	Weekly Action Steps

Weekly Planner

Week of: _____

SUNDAY

MONDAY

TUESDAY

WEDNESDAY

THURSDAY

FRIDAY

SATURDAY

to-do

notes

Scripture Promise

The Lord is my shepherd, I lack nothing. He makes me lie down in green pastures, he leads me beside quiet waters, he refreshes my soul. He guides me along the right paths for his name's sake.

Psalm 23:1-3

Week of:

I'm thankful for: My petitions & requests:

People on my mind:

Listening ...

Surely your goodness and love will follow me all the days of my life, and I will dwell in the house of the Lord forever.

Psalm 23:6

Today God spoke to me through:

☐ Jesus

☐ Scripture

☐ Holy Spirit (Still Small Voice)

☐ Circumstances

☐ Creation

☐ Dreams & Visions

☐ Believers (People)

☐ Praise & Worship

Confirming through Scripture

List Bible verses that agree: Do any conflict? ☐ Yes ☐ No

My response:

Actions to take:

God's faithfulness ... Revealed!

God-Given Callings
"Whom shall I send??"

My Goals, Callings and Ministries:

Weekly Action Steps	*Weekly Action Steps*	*Weekly Action Steps*
_____	_____	_____
_____	_____	_____
_____	_____	_____
_____	_____	_____
_____	_____	_____
_____	_____	_____
_____	_____	_____
_____	_____	_____

Weekly Planner

Week of: _____

SUNDAY

MONDAY

TUESDAY

WEDNESDAY

THURSDAY

FRIDAY

SATURDAY

to-do

notes

A Most Important Note

Jesus promises to send the Holy Spirit to guide us and comfort us (John 14:16). As you consider the many promises in this book, know that, as child of God, you can count on God to honor each one, confidently reminding Him of these treasures in your prayer life.

However, there is one important requirement: In order to receive the Holy Spirit and take hold of the precious promises, you must first be one of the body of Christ. That means you need to have accepted Jesus as the Savior and Lord of your life. This is what it means by "belonging to Christ."

The Way, The Truth and The Life

It all comes down to His Love for us, the gift of freewill, and a choice only we can make. God's chose to send His Son, Jesus, to ransom us *completely* from the penalty of sin — which is eternal separation from God. To be grafted into the wonderful inheritance of promises given by God in the Bible, we must *choose* to accept Jesus Christ as the Son of Almighty God, believe in His sacrifice, and accept Him as Lord of our life.

It is Our Choice to Make

"For God so loved the world that he gave his one and only Son, that whoever believes in him shall not perish but have eternal life." John 3:16

Sometimes, we make it harder than it has to be but the gospel message is quite simple: Believe that Jesus is the Son of God, sent by God to be a sacrifice, or a ransom, to pay the full price of our sin, which is eternal death and separation from God. Trust, then, in this same Jesus as our Lord and Savior, knowing that as He rose from the dead, we who believe in Him will follow and live eternally with Him.

There is no other requirement other than what the Bible tells us in John 3:16. This is the most important decision you will ever make.

Other books by Kelly Langston:

Last Request: A True Story of Faith and Redemption

When God Gives a Dream: Reaching Your Impossible Dream in God's Power

40 Prayers for Perilous Times: Powerful Intercessory Prayers for an Upside-Down World

Autism's Hidden Blessings: Discovering God's Promises for Autistic Children and Their Families

Do you have a God-inspired dream to become an author?

Today, God is pouring out stories—*incredible stories*—and it is time to get those stories out a world that needs His Light.

If you have been waiting to get your story out there, it's time to reach your dream of becoming a published author. Go to the following link where I share my publishing journey... and exciting tips to help you reach your dream!

www.inspirewritepublish.com

For more information about Kelly Langston and her books:

www.kellylangston.com

Made in the USA
Coppell, TX
01 March 2020

16370655R00181